Two Cats for Puerto Rico

By The Same Author

ISLANDS OF EXPERIENCE

A POET'S SKETCH
OF HIS BIOGRAPHY

KID ON THE RIVER

THE COPPER SANDS

THE N.P.M.W.A.R.A.

A SAILOR'S YARNS —
AND OBSERVATIONS

THE HIGHLINE TRAIL

ONE LIFE'S THREAD

Two Cats for Puerto Rico

Dean Nichols

Resource *Publications*
An imprint of *Wipf and Stock Publishers*
199 West 8th Avenue • Eugene OR 97401

Resource Publications
A division of Wipf and Stock Publishers
199 W 8th Ave, Suite 3
Eugene, OR 97401

Two Cats for Puerto Rico
By Nichols, Dean
Copyright©1994 by Nichols, Dean
ISBN: 1-59752-279-1
Publication date 6/27/2005
Previously published by Binford & Mort Publishing, 1994

For
Matt and Archie
and Jeff and Ken
    who built them;
and also for Bob
    who got them there.

The Lord on high is mightier
than the noise of many waters, yea,
than the mighty waves of the sea.
                    Ps. 93:4 KJB

Contents

A River Rat Goes to Sea 1
Warmer Down that Way 9
Made in the U.S.A. 15
The Sea Gives No Quarter 19
Cherish the Moments 23
We Enter the Tropics 29
Diamonds—We Own Them All 35
Cinco de April 39
Tehuantepec 47
A Siren Call 55
Waters of Four Nations 61
A Different Sleep Tonight 67
Path Between the Seas 71
Diversion to Paradise 77
Brutal 85
And Yet Brutal 89
The Taste of Victory 93

Acknowledgements

When I was presented this unique opportunity to take this voyage, and to write the story, I turned to my wife, Ramona, and said, "Well?"

And in her own, inimitable way, she answered, "You know you are going."

It is good to have a wife like that.

[The following is from the book, *ISLANDS OF EXPERIENCE*, by the same author.]

Far from being all romance and adventure, life at sea on a small boat can mean long, long hours of weary toil, and empty, yet full in their peculiar way, day upon day of infinite loneliness. Yet I find that the weariness is proof for that inner need to know that I have earned my pay; and the loneliness becomes the glass through which I see my life; the frame for the picture of my life; the necessary backdrop for the drama of my life; the illumination for the way of my life.

Because I Must

I'm alone on my ship as the salt sprays fly,
and the scattered clouds grace a clear, blue sky;
and a lonely eagle shares my cry,
as he rules his winged throne on high,
that this we know we must do or die.

I'll never know if the tireless sea
can be as lonely for him as it can for me,
or if weary hours dragging endlessly,
or if aching bones or back can be
the price he knows he pays to be free.

But I know the price, when a long, long run
has kept us going from sun to sun,
and my limbs grow weary 'ere the harbor's won;
and I feel all the loneliness of one
who knows he must sail till his life is done.

The blessing of life is toil, they say;
and my worn frame tells that I surely pay.
But the lonely hours are the searching ray
that frames my life, that lights the way;
and I know why I sail on the sea this day.
     November 30, 1965

Prologue

This is a true story; every dramatic episode is told as it actually happened. Presented here are the intimate, yet telling details of this unique voyage. But with all the earnestness I possess, I urge the reader to understand that the integrity of the telling demands such intimacy.

And this delivery voyage was also the shakedown cruise. The whole purpose of any shakedown cruise is to shake out problems, problems common to any building process. And a number of "problems" were indeed shaken out.

For seventeen long days, and over five thousand, five hundred miles, and stopping only three times for fuel, these two fast Catamarans raced down the eastern edge of the Pacific Ocean, skirted two Gulfs, raced across a continent through a world famous canal, charged out across the middle of a demanding sea, and slammed along the edge of another ocean.

And Capt. Bob Wengel? He was not paid by the day, or by the hour. He was paid to deliver these two small ships from the place of their birth in the Pacific Northwest to their new owners, the Port Authorities of San Juan, Puerto Rico. His pay did not even begin until they were docked, safely, at their new home. He had reason to push them—hard.

When Capt. Bob read the first draft of this story, he met with Matt Nichols, President of the Yard that built them.

He protested: "I didn't beat up your boats, Matt."

I agree. But that old Navy, Chief Bos'n did push them to their limits. All I am saying is, although he never pushed them *beyond* their limits, nor did he crowd his own Guardian Angel *beyond* his allowed margins, he surely left no slack. And, the fact that the ships, and we, survived that brutal run so well is living testimony to the knowledge, capability, courage, and solid determination of this young Captain.

Nowhere is it ever meant for this story to impugn in any way the integrity of the design, construction, or operation of these Australian-designed, Nichols-built small ships.

On the contrary, I saw this voyage as one confirming that integrity *all the way*. We made it, dammit; we made it. What more did you pay for, Matt?

But may I make here a personal disclaimer myself. I did *not* go on that remarkable voyage to "report on Bob Wengel." I went for the incredibly unique experience. And I wrote to tell that experience. And I told it, as it touched my eyes, my ears, and my nose, my guts, my heart, and my soul.

And if that telling exposes a bit more of that unusual and most capable young man than might be perfectly comfortable for him, let it be repeated—like us all, he is not perfect; he is a mortal human being. And again, I'll say again, as I shall repeat yet again in this story; the next time I have three million dollars worth of boats to send anywhere in the world, the first man I'll call will be Capt. Bob Wengel.

He owes no one any apologies. And I make no apologies for what I have written. Read this dramatic story, and make your own judgements.

Now, this man *is* a character. And characters make for much more interesting stories than do ordinary people. That is why, in the last paragraph of a cover letter I sent to him with the manuscript, I wrote: "You are a little different, Bob Wengel. But then, myself, being a Nichols, I know what it is to be 'a little different.' And I love it. [Again] we are so much more interesting than ordinary people."

Note: In this story, we shall use the Armed Forces' 24-hour clock, which has been adopted by most seamen. It is a good system, better than A.M. and P.M., I'm thinking, and is easily learned.

For example: 0300 hours is 3:00 A.M.; 0500 hrs—5:00 A.M.; 1200 hrs—noon. And then, 1300 hrs is 1:00 P.M.; 1930 hrs—7:30 P.M., and so on.

This story will be read by many landsmen; but by many seamen as well. And since it is a sea story, let us defer to the seamen.

    Capt. Dean Nichols
    24 August 1990
    2359 hrs—one minute before midnight.

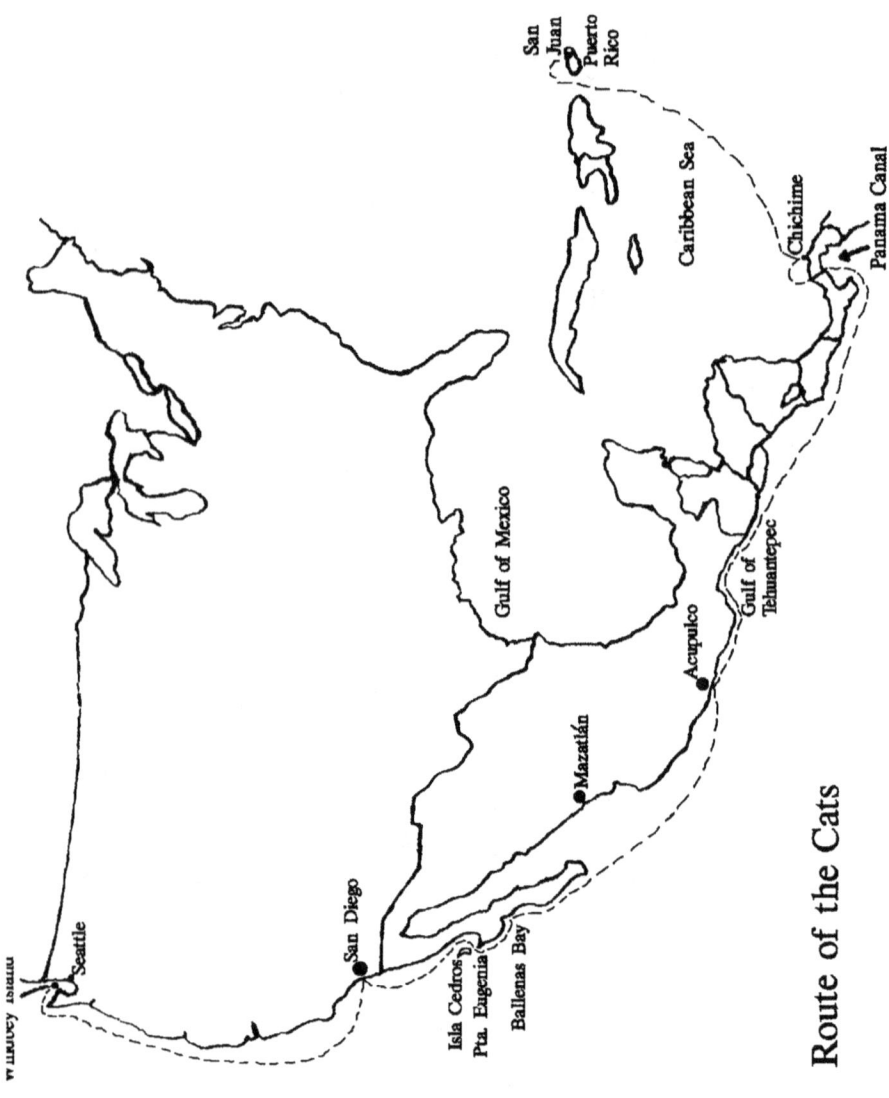

CHAPTER 1

A River Rat Goes to Sea

Day Two—It is a gray morning. The indefinite ceiling of 2 to 3 thousand feet is gray. The horizon, on this ball called the earth, draws its line but a few miles away, backed by that gray curtain. And even the silver sea, the sparkling, silver sea, this morning is gray.

Angry seas off the Oregon Coast.

The long Pacific swells, 4 to 7 feet, and rolling in on our starboard quarter, are making us yaw a bit. The helmsman, handling the well-designed, but manual, steering, is working. And the swells are building. The light chop, from almost square astern, although rocking us a bit now and then only makes the sea more interesting—except, when one would peak on top of a peaking swell.

I had said, "swells, rolling in...." But these Cats are more than prowling; they are loping along at some below their top speed, but still at 20 knots. We are outrunning those swells. And even when those slicing, narrow, twin bows now and then catch up with one of those above "exceptions," the sea gently but firmly reminds us of her power. That surfing run, which often reaches 26 knots down the forward faces of those swells, is markedly slowed for a few moments, to as low as 15 knots.

Designed in Australia by men who know the "wild and often angry sea," these 76-foot long, 29-foot wide Catamarans were clearly well designed.

Built by my cousins' shipyard, Nichols Brothers Boat Builders, at Freeland, on Whidbey Island, some north of Seattle, these boats show the true craftsmanship that is increasingly known and respected, even 5000 miles of busy, if not angry sea away. (The Puerto Rican Government, Public Port Authority wanted boats by this yard. It was that simple.) One has but to look at a weld, back in a corner there, or at the overhead hand rails, and see the attention given to thoroughness, fidelity, and unobtrusive strength. As I have often told others, "You can buy a cheaper boat; but you can't get more honest boat for your dollar than from this capable, small shipyard."

The sea is our friend, even our servant; but as it has been so well written, "She is terribly unforgiving of any carelessness, incapacity, [arrogance] or neglect." The sea is not yet angry, today, but she is very busy, and baring her teeth once in a while. I am poignantly aware of the singular fact that we are land animals. And if we are going to successfully challenge the sea, reap her bounty, travel her highways, we *must* be prepared. Our skills and knowledge must be thorough; our bodies and minds finely tuned; but most of all, we must ride a craft that is at home upon the sea. And these small ships are.

Capt. Bob Wengel, Commander of this flotilla of two, at age 46, has 20 years of Navy experience, beginning at age 17, and the following years running boats, some of this same design. Aboard our ship, the MV *Viejo San Juan*, he has three young, but quite capable, competent, and confident young men to help him. And that is good. They are: Mike Carroll, 27, Acting Mate; Kurt Helley, 33, Engineer; and Stephan Vlahovich, 22, Deckhand. And on the following ship is LaDell Ashley, 27, Skipper; George Ott, 26, Mate; Rex Lukinich, 36, Engineer; and Garrett Terwilliger, 21, Deckhand. Nine lives are riding this day on two aluminum cans, each pushed along through the buffeting waves by nearly 1000 eager, diesel horses, forcing the sea aside. The sea gives way, but she is also testing the metal of both men and machines. I'm glad I'm riding a Nichols-built boat today.

1100 hrs: The swells, still following from the starboard quarter, are now up to 7 to 10 feet, and the following seas, 2 to 3 feet. From the whitecaps, we can judge the following wind at around 16 knots. But at 20 knots, we are even outrunning the wind. And the narrow, twin hulls are giving us an easy ride. Two off-watch men are sleeping soundly on their foam pads on the steel deck. (I know they are aluminum decks; but steel sounds harder.) I think their sleep would not be so uninterupted were they riding a monohull at 20 knots over this lumpy, water highway.

And following obediently, half a mile behind us, our sister ship, the MV *San Geronimo*, is cruising as easily. Oh, she is obviously moving with the surface of the sea, but like our own, there is no pounding, no bone-jarring slam of hard water against a flat, metal hull. Once in a while, an extra wave will join one of

MV *San Geronimo* following on station, half a mile behind.
Note the reflection in the side glass.

those "exceptions," and the twin bows will throw that confused sea up against the under belly of the joining decks. The thunder of a drum is heard, but still the ride is soft and easy, and two men slumber blissfully on.

But how did this old river rat, this retired tugboat Captain, who also spent a few years in Air Traffic Control, come to be riding this racing Cheetah on a 5000-plus mile delivery run, from an island in the cool and fresh Pacific Northwest to a tropical island on the eastern edge of the Caribbean Sea?

Well, it helped to be a relative of the builders; it helped to be a man of the sea; it helped to be audacious enough to ask, and to still say, "Yes, I want to go," in the face of my cousin's warnings:

My first cousin's son, Matt Nichols, President of the yard, was speaking, "These are strictly passenger carrying, day boats, 'Uncle' Dean. There are no staterooms, no showers, no galley; no heat (They are built for the tropics, you know). There *is* a head with flushing toilet, and a tiny wash bowl, with a single, cold water tap. That is all. There is no hot water for shaving, so you'll probably wait 'til you get home. Your bunk will be a foam mattress, jammed down between two rows of seats; you will need your own sleeping bag. Your 'galley' will be a microwave oven, lashed to a piece of plywood, which will be lashed to the tops of two rows of seats. Your cook will be you.

"It is some over 1200 miles to your first stop, San Diego, 1400-plus miles to the next, Acapulco, and 1400-plus miles to Panama. Then it is over 900 miles out across the middle of the Caribbean Sea to Puerto

Rico. Unless the weather drives you in, there will be no other stops. The first three boats, of this order of six, have already been delivered. The term 'brutal,' has at times been applied to those voyages.

"Do you still want to go?"

"Matt," I responded, "I think you'll agree that, especially at my age, this would be a once-in-a-lifetime experience?"

He agreed, "Yes, it would be that."

So I simply said, "When do we leave?" And when the answer came, March 29, I said, "I'll be there."

1300 hrs: The swells, and seas are now up even more. Occasionally they combine to 10 to 12 feet. Sometimes I think this Cat could catch a scared rabbit, on some of the surfing runs down the faces of these swells. For all of the good words about this relatively soft ride, I'm glad we are running with the waves. It would indeed be a brutal ride north, against them; although Capt. Wengel just told me that he has run these ships at 20 knots directly into swells up to 10 feet. "Really, not too bad a ride," he said.

As alluded to earlier, the Puerto Rican Port Authority needed to upgrade, and speed up, their "Bus Service," across San Juan Harbor, and, I believe, to an outer island or two. When they found these Catamarans which, especially on short runs, were nearly as fast as a hydrofoil, but costing one-eighth, or less, of the price, they ordered six identical ships. They are the basic, standard design hulls, and, structurally, the same house, only single deck, and *no* frills interiors. With burnished aluminum in lieu of paint, and with a very small wheelhouse, only slightly raised, and tucked into the forward end of the superstructure, they are just not as beautiful as the two and three deck tourist-attracting models.

But, beauty is, as in this case, "in the eyes of the beholder." The Puerto Ricans are very happy with the performance of the three already delivered, and a million dollar saving on each ship can make the bottom line look mighty pretty too.

The contract for the six ships included delivery to Puerto Rico. At first, the practical thing seemed to be to just lift these light, aluminum, little vessels out of the water and onto the deck of a ship, or barge, and haul them down. But the shipping price was staggering. Further study revealed that, though still costly, it was far less so just to crank them up, and run them down on their own bottoms. And that is what we are doing. Capt. Wengel has delivered three, one at a time. This is the first flotilla of two. I think I heard him tell LaDell Ashley, Skipper of the *San Geronimo*, "If you want to go to San Juan, Puerto Rico, just follow me. I'll be following my old tracks."

The angry seas fight back as a Cat roars down the face of a giant wave.

1700 hrs: We are still about four hours north of Point St. George. We had to slow down for a little while. The *Geronimo* came surfing down the face of a 15-foot swell, and buried her bows twice in the back of the swell ahead. So they had to cut their engines, and let her rise out of the green water.

CHAPTER 2

Warmer Down that Way

Day One—But when did this voyage truly begin? At the beginning of time? When my father, Capt. Luke Nichols, and his brother, my Uncle Mark, started the Nichols Boat Works in Hood River, Oregon, over 50 years ago? When, some 20 years later, Cousin Frank left the Boat Works, moved north, and started building boats there, on Whidbey Island, some north of Seattle?

Did it begin some 10 years after that, when he had a heart attack and his sons, Matt and Archie, came in and began the remarkable expansion of the facility into the small, but world known, Nichols Brothers Boat Builders?

When did this voyage truly begin? When the ship was ordered; or building began? When sea trials were completed? Or even when a crew went aboard each craft and took command?

No, it was really none of these. It began at around 1400 hrs, this day, March 29, 1990. And how do I know? The looks on the faces, the shift in the conversations that revealed the subdued excitement in

Two views of our spartan wheelhouse.

each heart that said, "This is it; this is the first step of the journey. All else has been preparation; but now, our bows are pointed toward the open sea. When we clear the Ballard Locks, our propellers will not taste fresh water again until we leave the first set of locks on the Panama Canal, over 4000 miles down the long coasts of the Americas, the land to our port, and the vast Pacific to our starboard."

Yesterday, March 28, the crews gathered at the Nichols Brothers Outfitting Dock, at Langley, on Whidbey Island. We met each other, bought stores, stowed our gear, and selected our favorite sleeping areas among the rows of empty seats.

We left about 1730 for Ballard, through the Locks, and secured for the night at the Mobile Fuel Dock. But this was only the "shifting of berths" not yet the beginning of a voyage.

This morning each ship took on her maximum fuel load of around 5000 gallons; a faulty gear oil pressure pump was removed, a correction made, and the pump re-installed. We were ready. And as already said, about 1400, we backed out, turned, and entered the locks, to leave the fresh water behind.

As we were locking through there were a number of interesting tourists there. They asked some interesting questions. Of course, I was not bashful about using the opportunity to plug these boats, and the Nichols Yard. They received it well. One sharp, older man, in a gray suit, asked, "If we drive up there, could we get a tour through that yard?"

I answered, "You bet you can. The President is my cousin, Matt Nichols. Tell him that Dean promised you that Matt would personally give you a guided tour. You will be impressed with what you see and hear." And then we had some fun banter.

I asked him if we were headed the right direction for Puerto Rico.

He answered, "Yes, you are."

12   *Two Cats for Puerto Rico*

Leaving the quiet waters of Ballard Locks.

"Well," I bantered back, "Last night, a man directed us that way," and I pointed astern. "He said to go till the big water, and turn right. We did, but we ran into a floating, concrete bridge."

He shook his head, and said, "Oh, it's awfully hard to get good directions these days. He probably thought you said 'Renton,' when you said 'San Juan.' No, you're OK now. Just go through this canal, turn right and cruise northwest for several hours until the swells get big, turn left for about 4000 miles. When you come to a big ditch on your left, go through that to the Caribbean Sea, head east, northeast for about 900 miles, and that's Puerto Rico. You can't miss it."

We laughed; I thanked him, and we cast off lines for the last time for two and a half days. When I told Capt. Bob the story, he concurred, very seriously,

"That's right; south to the big ditch, then ENE to Puerto Rico. He was right on."

There *was* one last, short delay. Up along the outside of Whidbey Island, Capt. Wengel discovered that whoever packed his charts had missed two, detail charts, that he really needed. So we eased into the beach; Mike Carroll went off the bow, waded ashore, and ran up to Bob's condo for the charts. Ten minutes later, we were really on our way.

My not being part of the watch-standing crew, I was free to sleep the night through. Out past Anacortes, the night closed in, so I crawled into my "bunk." An hour and a half later, I felt the swells change. The motion of the ship told me that we had turned south. It had been cold, in that unheated cabin; but I smiled, snuggled down deeper into that down-filled sleeping bag, and thought, "We're headed south: it is warmer down that way."

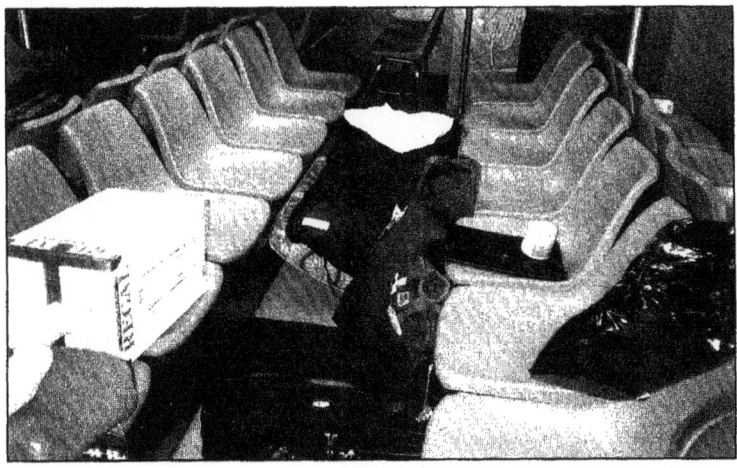

The author's berth for seventeen long days.

CHAPTER 3

Made in the U.S.A.

Day Three—Two purring Cats step swiftly over a settled sea. And that sea is shrouded by another gray dawn. The only white is that of the bones in our twin teeth, and the rushing, white wake that seems to be clinging desperately to its position some 20 yards back, where the blast from the twin props roll together.

We had rounded Point St. George in the night, and left the shallower water with its steep seas, well known to sailors of the south Oregon Coast. Although our course is generally south, we are claiming the Easting that the California coast allows and gaining some of the protection now from Cape Mendocino. And the water must be much deeper here. Though swells, 3 to even 5, and occasionally, 7 to 8 feet, still follow our starboard quarter, they are long, quite long. There are long races down the forward faces, and then only a slower climb over the long, sloping backs of the swells ahead.

One can see a smile on the face of each Cat, and almost hear the purring voices saying, "For *this* I was born." Twenty knots, and the governor controls are not full forward. Capt. Wengel says that we should be in San Diego by 0700 tomorrow morning. That's over 1200 miles, in under 60 hours. And at the roughest part, one could safely heat a bowl of soup in the microwave, and eat it at a plywood table.

Sixty hours; and I remember back, some fifty years ago, towing logs on the Columbia River from Hood River and White Salmon to Portland, 65 miles west, and running light back home. I was proud of our round trip delivery run of 60 hours—and 130 miles. Things have changed a bit, in 50 years. As someone wisely said, "*These* are the good old days." I'm glad to be alive this day."

1400 hrs: Our first sun, breaking through the clouds. And with it, the silver of the silver sea. The long, rolling swells are still following. But now we have added some 1 to 2 foot chop, also following. And the 15 to 16 knot following breeze is dressing the sea with occasional, small whitecaps. And two Cats are racing southward, ever southward, toward that historic canal.

Powered by two, 12V71 "Jimmys," and rated at some over 400 HP each, these are from a long line of "tried and true," two-cycle engines. And throttled back about 10 percent from their maximum cruise, they purr their contentment. They love to run, these Jimmys, but they don't like to be pushed. But back off, even a little bit, let them run easy, without that driving pressure, they respond with long hours of faithful service. Is that not also the same with man?

I'm not sure when the 6-71s (six cylinders, 71 cubic inches per cylinder) were first produced. But we used thousands of them in landing craft, and other uses, during WW II. For a long time, they were built in one, two, three, four, and six-cylinder models; and the pistons, dry sleeves, connecting rods, bearings, nozzles, and many other parts were interchangeable. And these 12V71s (12 cylinders in a V configuration) can, I understand, use those same parts.

Although Detroit Diesel, builders of these engines, is no longer connected to General Motors, agents for Detroit have told me, "Sure, call them Jimmys. It's a nickname the whole industry knows, and uses. Call them a 12-V-71 Jimmy, and anyone will know what you mean."

As I said, these are a two-cycle engine; that is, they fire on every downstroke, or one firing stroke every revolution. Turning these, as we are today, at a reduced speed of 1700 RPMs, 1700 revolutions per minute, times 12 cylinders, that is 20,400 firings per minute, or 340 every second. And that all makes for remarkably smooth running power. An electric motor cannot improve much on that.

And, they are made in America. Sorry, Deutz, but the Patriot in me likes that "Made in the U.S.A." label.

CHAPTER

4

The Sea Gives No Quarter

Day Four—San Diego, City of Yachts and Yachtsmen.

We are secured at the Standard Oil Dock in the Yacht Basin behind Shelter Island. The first leg of our long run down the coasts of the Americas is history. And moored here, we seem to be immersed in a sea of yachts—sailboats, runabouts, sailboats, gleaming white luxury yachts, and sailboats.

We will lay here a day, resting and giving our Engineers a quiet time to work on their engines. As said earlier, these Jimmys love to run, but they do respond to the caring touch. We have two good men, Kurt, and Rex, to do that.

The two crews walked the few blocks up to a restaurant, curiously called the Boll Weavil for brunch, and shared our stories. We found that the *San Geronimo*'s little "problem" with a couple of those steep, following seas was potentially quite serious.

Our lead ship,*Viejo San Juan* took on 2700 gallons of fuel, for that 1200-plus mile run, and the

San Geronimo, following, took on 2900 gallons. A following boat will always use some more fuel because they are frequently having to adjust their speed to keep station with the lead ship. It was probably one of those "adjustment periods" that contributed to their "problem."

Surfinq down the faces of those following seas, we were both repeatedly jamming our noses into the backs of the wave ahead. It was an exciting time, watching those valiant, narrow bows struggle a bit, deep in the green water, but always rise, part the water, and lead us over the back of that wave, ready for another surfing run.

But the *Geronimo* had been falling behind. So the Skipper added a couple hundred RPMs and about 2 knots to close up on her lead ship. That slightly increased speed, plus, no doubt, an "inconvenient" swell and sea combination, produced an extra pile of water; and the MV *San Geronimo* rammed her nose into that, deeply. And for just a little while the MV *San Geronimo*, Puerto Rican State passenger vessel, had over 8 feet of green water stacked on her foredeck.

But green water also carried back beneath, apparently filling the otherwise large airspace between the hulls, and tumbled a slug of water into their otherwise well-protected port engine room air vent. That salt water found a gap in a big L, just over the main generator and electric panel. When lights flashed and flickered, Rex, the Engineer, dove for his engine room and found lightning all over the place. He cleaned the place up, as best he could, in those surging seas; the generator set struggled on, burping and coughing, and slowly cleaning itself. A close one, but the sea gives no quarter. *We* must, and will, adapt.

Those following seas, though never as severe as those along that southern Oregon coast, stayed with us all the way to the Santa Barbara Channel. Fog threatened, but never really interfered, and we entered San Diego Harbor just as the deep gray grudgingly gave way to the dawn.

The refueling is complete. Capt. Wengel is shopping for groceries for a hungry crew; and the boys are cleaning up their grubby ships. And I answer questions, willingly, by the curious. These are indeed, unique ships. And they catch the eye of the discerning.

With our boarded-up forward glass, and simplified construction, we appear a couple of ugly ducklings in a bay full of swans. But I see not one swan out there who could stay in our wake as we charge off tomorrow for the 1400-plus mile run south to Acapulco. And I see not one that would allow her crew to casually heat a bowl of soup in a microwave oven, while her bows are slicing the lumpy, sloping seas at over 20 knots.

CHAPTER 5

Cherish the Moments

Day Five—The purring engines are moving two Cats, easily but swiftly southward, ever southward over the silver sea.

Curiously, I didn't sleep well last night. Oh, a harbor has its own comforting sounds: the ship nudges gently against a piling, a ramp guide squeaks, as the slow tide raises or lowers, and so slides its position in its grooves. A motor mutters its muted sound as a boat eases at "no wake" speed into or out of her berth. And on a small boat, where one sleeps below, the curious scratching sound of a propeller on a passing boat comes up through the hull, reminding the sleeping sailor he is indeed afloat in the protected waters of the harbor. Oh, sleeping in the harbor is sweet.

But, a sailor, like a ship, in the harbor is safe; but that is *not* what either was created for. With a good crew on watch, an able seaman at the helm, the off-watch sailor can crawl into his warm bunk and let the infinitely varied motions of the waters rock him to sleep.

And those special sounds at sea—the soft and whispering sounds, or the stormy, shouting sounds, speak a special language of peace into his sleeping ear. And on these most unique, eager, racing felines, he can even grin a peaceful grin as he feels the ship rise over the back of the wave ahead and go surfing down that forward face, shearing right or left. And he grins his sleepy grin, because, in his mind, he can hear the muttered grumbling of the helmsman as he cranks rapidly on the wheel, "Now come around, baby, come around. We don't want to go to Tokyo; we are headed for Acapulco." Oh, sleeping is good on a living ship at sea.

It was cold when we arrived in San Diego. We still appreciated the warm comfort of our down sleeping bags. Still, palm trees greeted our landfall, and palm trees will wave to us, now and then, when we close in on the shore, and palm trees will greet us at every landfall for the rest of our long voyage.

But this morning, the California sun was warm. Re-fueling was complete; minor repairs were completed; and Capt. Wengel, though firmly in command, and even curt and taciturn while wrapped in thought during the always many, last minute preparations, still was ever thoughtful of his crews. More than ample food was stowed into the lockers yesterday, and insulated chests were procured. This morning, he is buying ice for them. "As we move into the tropics," he said, "Our fresh things won't do so well without ice."

So far, we have had three minor casualties. Still, the Spirit has smiled upon us, protecting us from serious developments, but leaving us the warning that the sea *will* be respected. Shortly after the saltwater/electrical problem aboard the *San Geronimo*, Rex, the Engineer, was reaching into a filter area. His watch band touched the electrical connection on a heat sensor. Apparently, there were still some spurious voltages and amperages running around the engine room from that saltwater invasion. For the arc that formed slashed his metal watch band in two and blew the watch across the engine room. Only a very slight burn showed on his wrist. But, understandably, I had to pry the story from him.

But during that wild ride, off the southern Oregon coast, our Engineer, Kurt, making his "rounds" in one of the close-quartered engine rooms was caught momentarily off balance. The ship took a shear and then slammed sideways against 60 tons of heavy water. The water won, and Kurt was flung against a corner of a manifold. Today, the deep bruise on his hip, the size of a woman's hand, is a bit painful but not at all debilitating.

And yesterday, as we were loading stores, and as I stepped down onto a lower ledge on the edge of the deck to receive another handoff, my attention was momentarily diverted. My foot stepped on a single, one-inch poly mooring line. The line rolled, and I was over the side and into the water between the ship and the dock. Eager hands hauled an embarrassed old River Rat, dripping saltwater, out from San Diego Bay. Someone hosed me off with fresh water; I changed clothes, again (I had just shaved, washed up, and put on clean clothes) and we all walked up to

Where the author was "baptized" in San Diego Harbor.

the Chart House, where Capt. Wengel treated us to a fine dinner.

Today, a knee is a bit sore and a shoulder reminds me of a wrenching grab for a rail. But otherwise, we are all well and ready to sail. It is just that, yet again, the sea has warned us, "Stay alert; watch your step, have a corrective move ready, always ready, in the corner of your mental computer. I ask no quarter; I give none. And I often give no warning. Challenge me, and I shall reward you; but only at the price of vigilance."

1130 hrs: The crews all aboard, the engines warm and running, we slipped our moorings and eased out from the shelter of Shelter Island. A half hour later, we turned south, as the low, long, rolling swells from the Pacific, again from our starboard quarter, lifted our sterns and nudged us onward into Mexico. There was no line across the sea, as we stepped over. The sea does not recognize those lines. And the fish, and the whales, and porpoises recognize no lines. And the sea birds, and winds, and the clouds recognize no lines. Man can draw his lines, and we must, but only God can set the boundaries of the sea.

1330 hrs: And what can one say about this day? The following swells are long and low; the following, low chop is only occasionally gracing the surface with small whitecaps; a few white Terns fly by, ignoring the intruders, but gloriously flashing reflected sunlight from their white wings. The sun shines, but through a thin haze that softens the silver-blue of the water. And to the horizon, north, south, east, and west, there is not another craft. We are alone; the sea is ours. There are no "wars, or rumors of wars," there are no "earthquakes in diverse places;" there is no "famine in the land." "Cherish the moments," songwriter, Gloria Gaither warned, "Cherish them now; this day will never be again."

And so the day remained, even as the sun became a dark, red ball, and dropped behind the border of the western sea. Night closed in, a warm bunk waited, and, with the comfort of a good crew on watch, I crawled into that bunk, and let those "infinitely varied motions of the waters, rock this sailor to sleep." Oh, sleeping is good on a living ship at sea.

But just before I slept, I had spent a bit of time by the starboard rail, absorbing the beauty of a dark, clear night, with blazing stars overhead and a big half-moon, laying its rippling, yellow path across the rippling sea. And falling lower, as we race southward, Ursa Major, the Big Dipper, points to the great north star far astern, but a little to the port, telling us that we are, indeed, cruising southward, with yet that steady easting, carrying us under the belly of North America.

CHAPTER 6

We Enter the Tropics

Day Six—Under the belly of North America. Before the reader checks his globe, what city of the United States lies due north of the Panama Canal? San Francisco; Salt Lake City; Wichita; Washington, DC; Boston? How about New York City?

Yes, we have yet some easting to add to our southern run.

0300 hrs: There are lighted cities only a couple miles off our starboard beam. We are racing down, close under the lee of 20-mile-long Isla Cedros (island of the cedars). Although Capt. Wengel said that he was certain there were no cedar trees there. A curious name, then. In an hour or so, we will round Point Eugenia, and set our course even further east.

0330 hrs: The haze has cleared; the sky is ablaze with the brilliancy of the stars. The boys on the bridge have been thrilling to one meteor after another; some, they said, streaking across the full sky. And with her near 30-foot beam, the wide-set eyes, the running lights on the MV *San Geronimo*, following faithfully a quarter mile behind, make her look like a big ship bearing down on us.

0600 hrs: Dawn is rising out of the Sea of Cortez, the Gulf of California, and flooding over the mountains of the Baja Peninsula. And I remember the old, sailor's proverb: "Red sky in morning, sailors take warning. Red sky at night, sailor's delight."

For a brief time, there was a strong, deep red spread across 20 degrees or so of the eastern horizon and being reflected from the oily smooth waters. But it faded so swiftly, I almost wondered if it had really been there.

Well, we shall see. Was that old salts' proverb just for sailing ships? By 1800 hrs tonight we should be nearly 250 miles from here. Can that brief, so brief warning be for us? Oh, I can hear the other sailors say, "Weeel, it never hurts to be watchful." And our faithful, powerful, purring Cats rush on, southward, ever southward, down the long coasts of the Americas.

But a memory of the dawning clings. There was a distinct, slanting, black bar clearly dividing the red into two halves. Two lesser storms? Oh, but that is an old sea proverb.

My knee hurts when I bend it; my breast bones hurt; my shoulder sends a searing surprise through me when I reach over my head. Should I cry about these things? Or should I realize what the wise ones have found: that I am a privileged one; that the pains only point their fingers at the frailty of the flesh. But God is telling us, "Ignore the flesh; you are here to witness the Glory of My dawn."

The Nichols-built cruise ship MV *Sea Lion* in Ballenas Bay, Mexico.

1030 hrs: We hailed the *Sea Lion*, lying at anchor in Ballenas Bay, bay of the whales. She is one of the Explorer Class cruise ships, also built by the Nichols Yard on Whidbey Island. With her gleaming white, her triple decks, her classic lines, she looked the Queen she was, a luxury cruise ship. Beside her, our little, square ships, with their boarded up glass, looked so utilitarian. Ah, but *they* will be paddling around the bays, dispatching small boats full of tourists, looking for whales. And we, *we* will be racing for far away Puerto Rico, in another ocean, and—at over 20 knots.

We lingered near them, in the breathless, ocean air, and on a tranquil sea, while some of our crew shared banter with ones they knew aboard the big ship. Our Engineers used the quiet time to check their engines, add oil, and give them that most es-

The swan and the ugly duckling.

sential, caring touch. We were invited to dinner, but Capt. Wengel declined, "We have an appointment in San Juan that we are committed to keep."

So when our Engineers completed their work, we backed away, pointed our bows toward the southern seas, and raced away, leaving the swift streaks of our wakes behind us. And who will remember? Oh, but I shall remember. Three Nichols-built boats have met on the sea in a "far away bay with a strange sounding name."

1800 hrs: Bahia Magdalena, Magdalena Bay, where, according to Capt. Wengel, lies a favorite breeding ground for Gray Whales. We have seen none, during this entire, glorious day. But the two promontories, Mt. San Lozaro to the north, and Santa Margarita Island to the south, remind us, as they reflect the amber, afternoon sun, of the movie, *South Pacific*.

The Cats are happy. The only disturbance, if one can call it that, on the surface of the sea is 6 to 10 inch riffles from the 6 or 7 knot following breeze, and the very long, almost imperceptible ground swells, also still following. But the helmsmen have only to ease the wheel now and then to correct our straight run. And the Cats are rewarding us with an added 1 to 1½ knots, at the same power setting.

And we are, finally, truly in the tropics. The T-shirts, and shorts, and bare feet emerged on the younger men yesterday and on we "older" ones today. We will not sleep in down-filled sleeping bags this night. They will be far too warm. The tropics are telling us their story.

And I think that here, we might interject a confession. Because of no running hot water on these "Day Boats," I think most of the crew thought we might be free from having to shave for the duration of this voyage.

But in San Diego, Capt. Wengel produced a two-gallon, electric coffee pot, with its inner parts removed. In fifteen minutes, one can have two gallons of hot water; enough for a shave, and the rest, mixed with cold in the utility tub in the ladies room, and a thorough sponge bath was easy. Once we had gone that far, we put on clean clothes and looked the part we were playing, whether we wanted to or not, as representatives of a top quality, American Ship Building Facility. When Capt. Wengel emerged, shaved, bathed, and refreshed in new clothes, the rest of us soon followed the example.

Oh, this able young Captain can give orders, sharp, almost curt, to the point, but never abusive. He does more by example, a real worker, and one taking his responsibility as Commodore of this small fleet, very seriously.

A glorious, red, red sunset, spread over 90 degrees of the western horizon, lingered for half an hour or more, before losing its hold on the day. If omens have meaning, then perhaps the slanting, black bar, dividing the red this morning, did mean that that warning was cancelled. We shall see. But now, the light is gone for this day. We should be off Mazatlán at dawn tomorrow.

CHAPTER 7

Diamonds—We Own Them All

Day Seven—0130 hrs: The ocean is yet gentle tonight. And behind us, the *San Geronimo* keeps station beside a silver moonpath, across a blackened sea. Only a couple miles off our port beam, the low mountains of lower Baja, so dimly lighted by the yellow moon, rise out of that darkened sea. And overhead, faithful Ursa Major, points to an ever lowering north star, now lying well off our port quarter. Our course for waiting Acapulco is now, SSE by S, a quarter S.

And the sounds of our purring engines, the swishing, swift sounds of the sea's answer to our passing; the whisper of the wind we ourselves are making, all remind a sleepy sailor, "Go to sleep, my friend, go to sleep. But you will miss much that speaks in the night, while you are sleeping."

0200 hrs: A rotating beacon beckons on the shore; and the lights of a city speak of cantinas, and music, and friendly voices. But we rush on, leaving the Baja behind, and suddenly find ourselves in the open sea, 150 miles off shore. In a couple hours or so,

Mazatlán, far over the northeastern horizon, will send a distant call to us to come, but we shall not listen. We have a rendezvous with waiting Acapulco, and our eager, hungry engines, their fuel tanks lowering, rush now across this open sea. It will be 20 some hours before even these racing felines close the land again. *Go to sleep*, sailor. There's nothing to write about in the night.

0545 hrs: The open sea; and she graces us with a glorious sunrise. It is depleting my film supply. And some shorter, 3 to 5 foot swells, are rolling down from the Sea of Cortez and mixing with the low, following Pacific swells. Of course, the Cats are playing with the sea, but they are making the helmsmen work a bit with that manual steering and those tiny rudders.

0610 hrs: The sun, like a fiery dragon of the deep, leaped from the sea and ended the photography. I think I was reaching for my camera, and so missed the "green flash." But the Captain, who was at the helm at the time said, "Oh, it was there."

In about three more hours, Mazatlán will lie, fair on our portbeam; but, as I said, she will be far down the side of this curving ball, 150 miles away. If the weather stays clear, we still will not see the mountains of Mexico again rise from the sea until late this afternoon.

Cast loose from the shores of a small bay, on an island where they were built, these Cats were given but days before they were thrust before the mercy of the open sea. Even with their Cheeta speed, they could not now run for shelter in under 7 or 8 hours, should a storm arise. Ship and helmsmen, sea and seamen would battle it out together. I think I shall not call that a "red sky" this morning, but as it truly was, a glorious sunrise, full of promise.

0800: We have company astern: a large, blue ship, 7 or 8 miles back. I didn't see us pass one, so I suppose she could be gaining. For obvious economy reasons, most ships do not move that swiftly, but a few , express freighters cruise at 25 knots and he could be one. But they do so with 20 or 30 thousand horses, not eight hundred.

The *Queen Mary*, I believe, swung four or six propellers with some 50,000 horsepower.

0920 hrs: The baby blue container ship of the Maersk Line just passed us with a bone in her teeth. She is the first ship we have seen at sea on this voyage, except our own *Sea Lion* in Ballenas Bay. There are hundreds, if not thousands of ships on the world's oceans every day. But then, it is an awfully big sea.

1230 hrs: Although those mixing, following swells and seas are making for a more lumpy ride and the helmsmen are working again, it is still a glorious day. Scattered clouds grace a dusty, blue sky; the sunlight flashes from the faces of a million, liquid diamonds, none of which will ever grace a lady's finger. But here, who could put a price on their beauty; who could steal them away, and hide them in their treasure chest? No one, not the richest of Kings. And yet this day, we nine sailors, riding two tiny, aluminum cans over this lumpy sea, own them all.

1500 hrs: The mountains of Mexico have risen from the sea, right where they were expected to, 45 degrees or so off our port bow. But they have appeared a couple of hours sooner than I expected.

Flying fish are beginning to appear, now and then, leaping from the water and gliding away in a swift streak, as they escape this metal thing charging down upon them. And what has that to do with two Cats for Puerto Rico? I don't know; but they are there.

CHAPTER 8

Cinco de April

Day Eight—0200 hrs: We have rounded Point Telino, a point with rocky warnings, and turned yet further eastward.

"At night, give this place a wider berth," the Mexican version of the Coast Pilot warns. But, as Capt. Wengel forcast, we are in quieter waters now. A straight, 200 nautical mile, 10 hour run, to Acapulco, the lower foot of this second leg of our voyage. The contented rumble of two hungry, purring power plants seems to have added a subtle eagerness to their tone, as they sense the food that awaits them at the oil dock there. We rush, now east-southeastward, if not faster, then at least with that subtly noticeable eagerness. And behind us, the *San Geronimo* faithfully follows our wake down a yellow moonpath, across a peaceful sea.

Our crew are changing the watch. But I, privileged one, will sleep yet a little longer before the dawn. But I shall not crawl back "into" my bunk but rather stretch out on top of my thin blanket. The warm and humid, soft and caressing air of the tropics is coverlet enough. But this fresh sea air of the tropics is not the oppressive air of the jungle. The sea air, though warm, is washed and clean. It is always good to breath the air of the sea.

And that crystal clear air is leaving the sky ablaze with stars; the Milky Way spreads its twin paths across the crown of the heavens. And in the east, a brilliant morning star, rising over Acapulco, spreads its own dim, but distinct path across the moving sea.

Acapulco, historic city, has, according to the Encyclopedia, "one of the oldest harbors on the North American Pacific Coast, and is one of the 44 finest in the world, a semicircular bay covering about eight square miles...."

And Acapulco is now a tourist mecca for North Americans; mention Acapulco, and eyebrows raise, smiles of delightful envy respond.

But we shall but refuel our hungry ships, take perhaps a day of "R and R," have a real chef's meal or two ashore, and then we shall race away, southward, ever southward, down the long coasts of the Americas—Mexico, Guatemala, El Salvador, Honduras, Nicaragua, Costa Rica, and finally, Panama, a little more than 1400 miles deeper into the tropics. And our easting has carried us into Mountain Daylight Time. We lose an hour, just by crossing a line that man has drawn.

About 1100, we passed San Francisco. That is what the Chart told us—San Francisco, Mexico, a village some 70 nautical miles up the long, white beaches from Acapulco. Along the low rise, above the white surf, are miles and miles of cultivated orchards of palm trees in neatly ordered rows.

Farther back, smoke rises from a fire, evidence that man is there. And then the hot, dry mountains brooding over the land.

What can one grow on those mountains? What good can they be? Oh, but they give space to the land. Man is much more than just a physical being, walking at any one time on but a few square feet of the land. Man's real being is Spirit, and he *must* have space, just space, unoccupied space; for without that space, his Spirit dies. Oh, yes, we need the mountains and the space they give.

The sea has been especially kind to us today. The very long, low ground swells go unnoticed by crew and craft. And, light now on fuel, our racing Cats again give us an extra 2 knots or more at the same power settings.

About 1130, the Captain allowed a tension relieving war to erupt between the two racing ships. We slowed; the *San Geronimo* came rushing up alongside, and then, full power on our own, two serious vessels of the Puerto Rican Merchant Marine jockeyed and sparred, as the two, young crews traded salvos of water filled balloons. As with most wars, hundreds of rounds were fired. Few hits were scored. Now, we can cruise sedately into Acapulco Harbor.

1230 hrs: As we lope easily along, east-southeasward under the tropic sun, beside a golden beach, white with surf, I am mindful of the crew in command of this ship. I have grandchildren, the ages of the Engineer, the Mate, and Deckhand. And the Captain is the age of my youngest daughter.

These young men are in command: and it bothers me not at all. I have paid my dues. Now, I ride as their guest, help a little now and then, and write their story. *Tempus fugit*—time flies. These eager, capable, competent young men do not know it now, but in fewer years than they realize, they will be where I am, and will be saying, "Wasn't it just a few years ago, we made that voyage to Puerto Rico? Where now have these new, young men come from?"

The view from my lofty position of years is good. I enjoy the view.

The seawall at Acapulco.

Cinco de *April*

Close to 1300 hrs, on this *cinco de* April, we slipped through the narrow channel between the Isla Roqueta and the mainland. Capt. Wengel slowed to half speed, out of courtesy to the number of small boats at anchor near the mainland shore. But once clear, he couldn't resist shoving the governor controls to the wall, and two Cats for Puerto Rico raced into the outer harbor of Acapulco Bay like a pair of Navy Fighter Jets, giving slack to no one. If the hundreds of pairs of eyes in the hundreds and hundreds of apartments, condos, and hotel rooms, blanketing the hills around this harbor, if they were not impressed, they should have been.

We eased into the inner harbor, and tied to the seawall of the main ship terminal. Courteous officials came aboard and assisted in the completion of a sheaf of papers. Capt. Wengel's agent, a very competent, courteous, young man, speaking excellent

The officials check our papers across the "chart table."

English, had not received the telex telling of our arrival time and need for fuel. I think Capt. Wengel hoped to be away by this evening. But, *"Mañana, Señor, mañana."* If fuel arrives in early morning, we should be away before noon, for that next 1400 nautical mile run down to the "Big Ditch."

These have been a glorious three days, with those "fair winds, and following seas."

1600 hrs: The rest of the crew have gone "scouting the town." I have stayed to guard the ships; and listen to the sounds, the unhurried sounds of a port dock in the tropics. And I hear the gurgle and lap of water between the ship and quay, and the squeak of the fender tires, as the residue of the ocean swells reaches us and sends the ships surging gently against their lines. The sounds of the sea. Such music to the sailor.

1800 hrs: The Captain generously invited an eager crew, now in fresh, clean clothes and washed faces, to dinner. We took a pair of cabs a couple of miles around the bay to a fine restaurant and dined, really dined. A few of us worked through the laborious process of making a telephone call home. The younger ones insisted we "do the town," and so we did, for an hour or two. But we were way too early; the night life in Acapulco does not really begin until 2300 or later.

Sitting in chairs, on the soft, sandy beach of this tropical bay, with the warm, soft breeze caressing our faces, the crew debated their next move. But Capt. Bob, because he is older and wiser, and because he had vital work on the morrow, and a crew to

Cinco de *April*

The sovereign flag of Mexico flies over palm trees
and stone at Acapulco.

direct, elected to go to our ship and a waiting bed. And I, because I am older and wiser, came with him.

The geology of the earth touches even this story. The North American Continent is tipping to the east, very slowly, but very, very definitely. As a consequence, where once were deep valleys, the East Coast now has long, deep inlets, bays, and coves, by the hundreds. But the West Coast, except where it has been torn by some more local geologic event, has none. Really good harbors are few, and the distance between them, far.

Acapulco Harbor, jewel of the southern Mexican coast, is one of the few. The entrance to the outer bay is wide, but also deep. There is no bar. So it can be safely entered, even during a storm. And the north half of the bay is protected by a 2 or 3 mile long, high, rocky hook. No crashing seas could penetrate that stoney wall. And we lie at the quay, across from but well up behind that protective hook.

Capt. Bob and I laid ourselves down on top of those soft beds, the Latin sound of music from a nearby cantina singing us to sleep. And curving around that hook, the dying energy of swells that began, perhaps 5000 miles away in the Gulf of Alaska, surge deep into the inner harbor of Acapulco. And two Cats for Puerto Rico, their purring silent for the time, surge with those dying swells and tug firmly at their lines.

CHAPTER

9

Tehuantepec

Day Nine—The Captain is smoking; and not cigarettes.

Yesterday, he had been promised fuel for 7:00 AM this morning. This morning he was promised fuel for 10:30 or 11:00. At 11:00 he was told that the supplier was out of fuel. It would be after 3:00 PM. And that was when that old, Navy Chief Bos'n came off the deck. He walked up to his agent's office and, I have no doubt, spoke a language other than cultured English, and it wasn't Spanish.

Oh, I know, the Mexicans have long ago learned how to handle irate Captains. But they were completely blown off course by the storming fury of a United States Navy, Chief Bos'n's Mate. And in little over an hour, two tank trucks drove up, ready to pump fuel. Those "fair winds, and following seas" are being wasted today, out on the "peaceful" ocean. Had fuel, as "Plan A" had called for, been available, and we could have sailed at dawn today, this hour would have found us around 160 miles down the long, southern coast of Mexico.

But the Latins have a cultural facet that almost demands that they say, or promise what they believe the other *wants* to hear. You ask, hopefully, "And we *will* have fuel at 7:00 AM?"

"*Sí, Señor*, at 7:00AM."

And when it does not arrive, and you ask, "Where is my fuel?"

The hands are spread, the tone of voice implies that surely, you *must* understand, "But *Señor*, the tank farm is dry. The supply truck does not arrive today," or some such answer. And it all implies that, surely, *Señor*, you must understand. But a Navy Chief Bos'n is not programmed to "understand" if a sailor responded to an order with *"Mañana*, Chief, *mañana*. Surely you understand."

It is hot today as most of us wait for the Engineers to complete their messy task. The Captain is hot, although able and willing to keep his sense of humor close to hand. And even the Coca Cola is hot, this morning's ice not yet having had time to do its work. I think LaDell made the most quotable quote of the voyage when, pulling back a wrapper, spoke, "Even the Twinkies are hot."

The *San Geronimo* was lying outside of us. We could refuel her starboard tanks; but there was not enough hose to reach on across to her port tanks. So that smoking Chief Bos'n turned her around, port side to. He never had a *"Tiger by the tail."* He had a Cat by the jaws, and she well knew it. I told him later, "I'm sorry you are under such duress, Chief, but I love to see snappy boat handling. That was good." He did not respond, but I caught just a flicker of that sense of humor "close to hand."

Tehuantepec

Leaving our soon-forgotten wakes in the peaceful waters of Acapulco Bay.

1700 hrs: Engine oil changed, fuel and oil filters changed, air locks cleared from the fuel lines, engine oil topped off, we slip our lines from the quay at Acapulco and point our bows to the waiting, open sea. And two fast Cats race away before the eyes of the "rich and famous," in their carpeted, costly condos, on the hilly shores of Acapulco Bay.

But the swift, definite streaks of our wakes will fold into the sea, and in but moments, leave not a trace of our passing.

And so it will be with the memory of nine sailors who, for a few hours, stirred the waters of the cantinas in Acapulco. And one may ask of them, and a waiter will answer, "The *Norte Americanos* from the swift ships? Who knows, *Señor*, who knows? Another Marguerita, *Señor*?" Memory of us, like our wakes, will fold into the sea of unrecorded history and leave not a trace of our passing.

The Chief Bos'n, correction—our Captain—is smiling now. The deck of a good ship at sea rises beneath his feet, the helm responds to his touch, and the end of the road, San Juan, grows closer by the mile. Oh, to be moving out upon the open sea is good. But our mission is to deliver, not cruise. The true reward, "Well done, thou good and faithful servant," will not come until our lines are secured to the quay in yet far away San Juan, on the Island of Puerto Rico.

"Heading one, zero, three, for one, two, one point five nautical miles." The Captain's terse message, with meaning for only one, brought an even more terse response on the radio from the following *San Geronimo*, "Roger, one, zero, three."

Our photogenic and good-natured Engineer, Kurt Helley, relaxing amid the organized chaos of our crew quarters.

Our course is only a few degrees east of SE, carrying us deeper, under the belly of the Americas. And incredibly, we are yet blessed with following seas, and light, following breezes, and with yet the long, low ground swells nudging our starboard quarter. The Cats are happy and running with an easy stride.

1800 hrs: We are, understandably, in a race with time. Every day at sea, or in port, costs money. And Capt. Wengel has commitments for, I believe, the 15th. So I was curious, while studying the chart just now, why his projected course around the Gulf of Tehuantepec kept us close to the land. We will be cruising for a while, as high as 61 degrees magnetic, or roughly ENE. It would be a much shorter route straight out across the Gulf. So I asked him.

"Well," he said, "Far too often here, the 'longest way round is the shortest way home.' Gales from the north, called, in the course language of the sailors in this area, 'Tehuantepecers,' can come up with little or often no warning. A ship, even a large ship some distance offshore, can find herself almost suddenly fighting short, steep seas, and 50 or 60 knot gales. When we stay tucked close in under the lee of the land, we can escape at least the buildup of those seas. But here; I'll let you read about it in the *Sailing Directions*."

And so, quoting from Publication 153, *Sailing Directions For The West Coasts Of Mexico And Central America*, Defense Mapping Service, U.S. of A., Fifth Edition, Page 76: "Winds and Weather:—In the vicinity of the Gulf of Tehuantepec, which includes Puerto de Salina Cruz, northers are particularly strong because of the damming of the N flow of air by the mountain ranges both to the E and W of the gap which lies immediately N of the head of the gulf. These gales, known locally as Tehuantepecers, generally prevail from October through April, and at times blow with a force that exceeds force 8 on the Beaufort scale. [50 to 60 knots] There is less than one day per month, of such winds, from May to September. The gales may last for several hours or for several days. They are liable to raise a very short high sea, and may be felt up to 100 miles offshore. The onset of these gales may be marked by a brief period of rain from arched squall cloud followed by quickly clearing skies, or the sky may be cloudless throughout. The barometer cannot be relied on to give any prior warning."

I am familiar with a similar phenomenon in Prince William Sound in winter, when the heavy, frigid air over interior Alaska squirts through the narrow gaps in the mountains ringing the northern boundary of Prince William Sound. Winds well over 100 MPH are recorded every winter.

And here, where a high pressure system in the western Gulf of Mexico can pile against the lower neck of Mexico, and that combine with lower pressure in this Gulf, this can make of the worn simile, "air escaping from the open neck of a balloon," a screaming reality.

I heartily agreed with our prudent Captain; the longest way round could well be the shortest way home. My respect for this able, young Captain grows daily.

But it is this gap, this lowland across the narrow neck of lower Mexico that has drawn engineers to study the feasibility of digging a sea level canal across this lowland.

Oh, so called "Environmentalists" would have a grand time decrying the "horrors" of the "disasterous mixing of the ecology of two oceans." But they are wrong. There is no disastrous mixing at Cape Horn, or across the Arctic. Water mixes, both ways, at the Ballard Locks in Seattle. Ships carry barnacles, sea lice, plankton, and much other sea life from sea to sea.

And the flow through that canal? There are highly qualified hydraulics experts who insist it would be little or none. But even if locks were required to prevent mixing or excessive flow, they would be low-level, single-lift locks, two, or three, or even four wide at each end, since there would be an inexhaustible supply of water—the sea itself. In the dry season, Panama has a serious shortage of water for their lock fillings. Of course, they waste much, with the many fillings and emptyings of their lock chambers, with no ship in the chamber. But that's another story.

And the Mexicans? They are our neighbors, good neighbors; they are fully capable of operating that canal. And the substantial income would tremendously benefit this poor country, our close, close neighbor on our southern border.

The locks, of course, could be built to handle the very largest of super tankers, which the present canal locks cannot do. I asked a very knowledgeable official there, why they did not build larger locks.

But he referred again to the dry season shortage of water. There would just not be enough water for larger locks. "We barely make it through the dry season now," he said.

And the savings in shipping time by using this low-level canal around 900 miles north of Panama? On a passage from New York to San Francisco, a ship would save close to 1800 miles. And such are the facts of economics—when one saves, we all are richer thereby.

But, politics, economics, ecology, and engineering are really not part of this story. We tell here, only the simple story of the voyage of two Cats for Puerto Rico.

CHAPTER 10

A Siren Call

Day Ten—A yellow-orange sun rises, where? Fifteen degrees off our starboard bow, and bathes the mountains of Mexico, close on our port beam, and the surface of the silky sea with its yellow-orange light. And a yellow-orange pathway from that rising sun seems to be nudging us closer under the lee of the protecting shore. We are skirting east-northeastward, around the Gulf of Tehuantepec. A light chop only comes to us, down that pathway of the sun.

All catamarans seem to respond to a light chop from any point well forward of the beam, and these two Cats for Puerto Rico skip eagerly forward. The chop seems to break the internal tension of the water, a mysterious drag upon a ship that occurs, incongruously, when she rushes over the deceitfully smooth surface of a glassy sea.

I believe it is essentially this principle behind the development of the bulbous bow on larger ships. That bulb protrudes forward from the bow stem, a short distance below the surface. The liquid "fibers" of that inner tension are shattered, if only for a few moments, and the remainder of the ship finds herself passing with less resistance through that incredibly complex, but so innocent appearing liquid, water.

And Tehuantepec smiles her innocent, inviting smile that says, "Oh, come now, Sailor. Come out upon my bosom today. See, I am smiling. I shall give you safe passage."

And I remember the warnings from the Good Book, to the fiery hearts of the young men, "Run, run from the seductive arms of the strange woman. Her lips are sweeter than honey, but her bed..."

No, Tehuantepec, we shall not give you the opportunity to turn your tempting siren call into a taunting jeer. We tread upon the sea by Divine permission, we know. We shall not "tempt the Lord our God." And Tehuantepec snarls, and bares her teeth with quickly increasing seas, 2 to 3 feet, and white caps on nearly every wave. We shall hold to the land.

0800 hrs: It has been well written, "Hell hath no fury like a woman scorned." Tehuantepec is giving her answer to our scorning. The seas now slamming us from 45 to 50 degrees off our port bow are now up to 5 to 7 feet; and the wind driving them, up to 35 to 40 knots. Every wave is capped with white; all our port sidelights are repeatedly washed with drenching, salty spray.

Capt. Wengel is personally conning the ship, and has not eased back a single notch on the governor controls. He seems to be saying, in effect, "You want to run, Cheeta? Then buck and run." And buck and run she does. And I just saw the *San Geronimo*, keeping station 250 yards off our port stern, lift her port hull out of the water, a full third of the way back. "Fair winds and following seas?"

"Not today," says Tehuantepec. "You scorned my seductive smile. My bed was soft and warm, and smelled of perfume. You scorned me, sailor, *me*. And the passion I was ready to give you has now been turned to fury. It is your own doing, fearful sailor, your own doing."

But Wisdom calls, down the long halls of time, and reminds him who has ears to hear, "Listen not to the temptress. Listen to Me, and hold yet a little longer to the shelter and lee of the land."

0900 hrs: And turning steadily to the right, along the northern edge of this Gulf, we find the seas already some abaft the port beam. Our ride is easier now. And I have time to look at those short, steep, 5 to 7 foot seas, and remember back, those long, long years ago to a tiny tug and the short, steep and deep seas on the Columbia River. Were it not for the distance to the land, and the taste of salt in the flying spray, I could be there again, running light for home and glad that my fragile rafts of logs were secure in a protected cove.

0930 hrs: Last night, the Captain told me of Tehuantepec; and this morning, she told me with her own words. I'm glad we listened to Wisdom, and held to the lee of the land. But already, in our curving run, the shouting wind, and the seas she is making, are coming to us off our port quarter. The ride is *much* easier now. It is time to have a bowl of cereal for my breakfast.

1015 hrs: The seas again are following, and there is not a fleck of white on the surface of the salty sea. Tehuantepec, with her painted eyelids, and her seductive smile, must wait for a less wise, young sailor to come along. And we, we rush on, knowing that her memory of us, like our wakes, folding into the sea, will leave not a trace of our passing.

1100 hrs: There must be another hole in the mountain wall to our left. A 25 to 30 knot wind is slamming the short, steep chop of a confused sea, broad on our port beam. But this racing Cat just shortens her stride a bit, to better catch the uneven trail.

1110 hrs: This is indeed an unpredictable place. In 10 minutes, wind and waves have swung 45 degrees to the right; and though we are a bare 2½ miles off the beach, they have blown up a short, mean chop from which the wind is again picking off the tops and throwing a drenching spray against our port sidelights.

1140 hrs: The water is green, bright green. The long, Pacific swells, unnoticed by us, are breaking in the shallows of the sandy shore, a mile or so off our port beam. And the streaming, offshore wind is catching their coronas and flinging them back, and high, with an awesome, white display. Tehuantepec is not finished with us yet.

1430 hrs: Would any reader believe, "fair winds and following seas?" In just a few hours, we will leave the Mexican waters and enter the offshore waters of Guatemala. Right now, 440 miles out of Acapulco, added to the 2600 of the first two legs, means that we have raced over three thousand miles down, down the long coasts of the Americas. And again, it is like a refrain, to say, "The following swells lift our starboard quarter, the following breeze dresses the sea with occasional whitecaps, and two happy Cats race southeastward down the long, long coasts of the Americas."

CHAPTER 11

Waters of Four Nations

Day Eleven—Sunday, April 8, 1990: "Six days thou shalt labor...." Ah, but is this labor? And if it is, even so, "Which of you, having a calf...?"

The instructions in The Book are firm and wise; but they are also prudent. We shall rest when we can rest.

0200 hrs: What is there to see in the dusty, dark night? Overhead, and off our starboard quarter, a nearly full, dusty yellow moon lights a dusty, clear sky, but gives us almost no moonpath at all across a glassy sea. Off our starboard beam, nothing but a close, dark night; off our port, the dusty, dim outline of the shores of Guatemala. I open a side window, and my face meets the heavy, humid, tropic night air. And that is curious. With our air conditioner keeping it cooler in the cabin, our instruments tell us that our *inside* air is heavier, and the relative humidity is higher. But when I opened that side window, my face met the "heavy, humid, tropic night air."

We are in Guatemalan waters now; but the night cares not at all; the sea cares not at all; and that "heavy, humid air" cares not at all. And our faithful, tireless engines care not at all, as they turn the balanced screws, pushing our knifing bows, and parting the glassy sea just enough to allow our quiet passing in the night.

These marvelously designed, and faithfully built machines are not meant to plane or rise up and ride on top of the water. The twin hulls are narrow and sharp, and, as I said, part the sea just enough to allow our passing.

The white, foaming bow wave on a "conventional" ship is wide. But along the sides of these twin, knifing hulls, it is close and narrow. As my face felt the warm 20 knot breeze, we ourselves are making, I saw our narrow, rushing bow wave, close alongside, and that, how like a horizontal waterfall, rushing for a union with our white wake.

What can one see, on a dusty, dark night, on a glassy sea, off the shores of this Central American country? Much, one can see much, if one has the "eyes to see," and the "ears to hear" the voice of the Spirit, Who gives the words for the pen to write. Oh, the pen indeed is mightier than the sword; but it must be pulled from its scabbard, and swung with all one's might, if it is to cut through a dusty, dark night, on a glassy sea, and spell the beauty that He has placed here, whether there be one to see, or hear, or write of it, or not.

But that is the beauty side, the spiritual side, of the night; the side that gives purpose to life. If one never sees beauty, how pointless would be our living.

But there is the natural side too. We *must* see where we step; we must eat, and rest, and refresh, and train our very natural bodies and minds, or we would never see the beauty. And the marvelous technology that our God-given minds have in turn given us make our passing in the night safe, and sure. Our radar is our eyes; our compass is our guide; our charts tell us, in graphic detail, what *should* be out there. And the training, and experience, and very real concern of our young Captain, puts it all together to determine exactly where we are, though we look out and see nothing but a dusty, dark night.

Oh, DR (Dead Reckoning) takes our speed, and direction, and tells him where we *should* be; our Sat Nav (Satellite Navigation) confirms where we are. But above all, it takes the competent, alert, attentive mind to make this a safe passage, so that I, the swordsman, can record the beauty of this midnight hour.

1000 hrs: So swiftly are we flying southeastward, that our propellers have tasted the waters of four nations in the night and dawn of this day—the offshore waters of Guatemala are far astern; El Salvador; and then the Golfo de Fonsica, where the narrow neck of Honduras finds a port on the Pacific Ocean, lies astern.

And we are now some 50 miles off the coast of Nicaragua. And the horizon, only 8 to 10 miles away on all points of the compass, wraps a perfect circle around us. And we are not giving Nicaragua an especially wide berth for other than the simple axiom, "A straight line is the shortest distance between two points." We are aiming for the bulge on the N.W. coast of Costa Rica.

No, there are no guns, no rockets firing our way. But Nicaragua is not letting us pass without some buffeting. A brisk east wind is driving a mean, 3- to 4-foot sea at us, 30 degrees off our port bow. And it is combining, at times, with the 4- or 5-foot, though long swells, coming at us square on our nose. Frequently, when those two combine, this Cat leaps for the sky, and for a brief moment, her sharp forepaws claw the air before knifing back into the sea. And still, the only pounding is when the twin bows now and then throw a ton or two of water up against the belly of the forward deck.

Capt. Wengel is steering now, or perhaps I should say, that old, Navy Chief Bos'n is conning the ship. I can see that subtle twinkle at the edges of his eyes that again is saying, "You want to run, Cheeta; OK, buck and run." And she is surely doing both this hour.

[And when did the landsman's term, "drive," slip into nautical terminology? One "runs" or "operates" a boat; one "drives" a car, or a truck, or a team of mules.]

"Fair winds and following seas?" Not today, off the western coast of Nicaragua.

1400 hrs: "Balmy south seas cruising; tradewinds sighing in the rigging. With our twin running sails drawing strongly, we sometimes almost surf, to 10 or 12 knots, as the long, following swells lift our stern, and nudge us forward before they roll under us. They will reach Bora Bora, long before we do. Ah, but who cares? *Mañana, Señor, mañana.*"

And that last is from the book, *Cruising The South Seas Under Sail. Not* this day, 50 miles off the coast of Nicaragua. The wind, possibly at 45 knots; certainly over 35 knots, is driving 8- to 10-, and frequently 12-foot, often breaking seas before it, and quartering us off our port bow.

The Captain has not called for slowing of our engines, so this racing, bucking Cheeta is *leaping* about, both fore and aft and side to side. All movement about the ship is from handhold to handhold, except when crossing the deck aft of the last row of seats. With no handholds there, a man does a sailor's hornpipe to get across. The soup would not do well in the microwave today. But then, these are not two, cruising sailboats, running before the tradewinds, downhill to Bora Bora. These are two Cats for Puerto Rico, still doing 20 knots and into a quartering sea. Although this is an incredibly exhilarating ride, the word "brutal" does come to mind. And we have not yet crossed the Caribbean Sea.

1600 hrs: We have turned to the right 10 degrees or so. The seas, though still mean, are now coming at us broad on our port beam. This "flat riding" catamaran is rolling almost 15 degrees, at times. But still, the ride is easier. And my nose confirms the fact. A hungry sailor is successfully cooking in the microwave.

1753 hrs: Another red ball just pulled its upper limbs beneath the waves. I watched closely for the green flash, but it was not there. I think the sea haze was too thick to let that delicate but often brilliant phenomenon through.

And off our port beam, we close the land of Costa Rica. The sea is again a peaceful pond. It should be good sleeping for the off-watch sailors tonight—and for me.

CHAPTER 12

A Different Sleep Tonight

Day Twelve—0500 hrs: The soft colors, of the diffused light of dawn, rises over the N.W. coast of Panama. Overhead, a pale, blue sky sends its own soft light down, to be reflected by the gentle waters. Only the very slightest of riffles appear on an otherwise mirror sea. Rolling slowly in from the South Pacific, low, long and easy swells alone remind us that we are indeed sliding down upon the ever moving surface of the sea. All around, or especially ahead, and to port and starboard, towering cumulus buildups speak of thunder showers to come. When I first looked toward the land, two towering cumulus clouds looked exactly like volcanos. But swiftly they changed their shape, and reached rapidly for the sky.

The Cats are happy; the gentle sea has given us an easy passage through the night. We should be secure in the still waters of Balboa Harbor by this evening; and our long run down the long coasts of the Americas will be over. We shall refuel our hungry engines, catch a bit of rest on the unmoving shore, and then run for 49 miles (from sea to sea), NNW through the fresh waters of that historic waterway.

The French had given up on its building, and a tiny insect, a mosquito, almost stopped the indomitable energy of our young nation; but we didn't give up. And yet today, this engineering achievement still serves a needy world. Made in America, or by America—that still has a rich sound.

We have gotten a little fat, and have relaxed our tenacious grip on freedom; and the very real slavery of hedonism has weakened the fabric of this great land. But she is still a great land. Regain her moral fibre, and she will quickly be a great, great land again. "Made in America." That does have a rich sound. And two made-in-America small ships race on on their delivery run to far away Puerto Rico.

The towering cumulus are closer now. I missed some thundershowers through the night, but surely, there will be thundershowers, washing the salt from our decks before we make our landfall tonight.

0830 hrs: Punta Ursula, on the Isla Jicorita; we turn due east. ETA Balboa City? 1930 hrs or so tonight, 220 nautical miles further on. "If the winds leave us alone," the Captain said. The quartering headwinds, and seas of yesterday cut our speed by as much as 3 knots. Even the following swells and seas, if too steep, markedly cut our average speed, because they make us yaw around. But now, a light breeze, a light chop, make for easy, happy running for these nimble ones.

1200 hrs: We are growing weary. It has been a long, long ride down the long, long coasts of the Americas. The sea has been kind, but she has given her warnings too. For most of the voyage, she has let us step lightly over her rippled surface. But there have been enough times where she made us work hard, if not fight, for our passage. And we are growing weary. It will be good to rest in the stillness of a harbor tonight.

1230 hrs: We *are* in shark-infested waters now. The boys on the bridge have seen seventy or eighty, some swimming, with that telltale fin out of the water, and arrogantly crossing our bows. And we just saw two, almost pacing us, not 30 feet off our port beam. We do not wish to swim in the fresh, green sea today.

1830 hrs: We are here; we have made it. The lights of Panama City, Balboa, the Naval Base, *the* Canal, blaze around the forward horizon. The guardian islands of the Archipelago de Las Perlas, pass swiftly by in the dark, close, close on our starboard beam.

The Captain is letting his eager steeds have yet a slack rein. And one can feel their eagerness, as they sprint for the finish line. But yet a little while, Cheeta, we are nearly there.

Tomorrow, we shall cross a continent, and then press out, northeastward across a new and open sea. But this long, long, long run down the coasts of the Americas is over. We have made it; we are here.

1930 hrs: We have dropped our hooks into a good, holding bottom, behind an island, a mile or so offshore. Contact with Officialdom has been made by radio. Now, we wait. And we can start to relax, and let the subtle, but necessary tensions that keep us alert and attentive to the passage, we can let them go. We shall sleep a different sleep tonight.

2400 hrs: A Pilot just came and took us the 2 or 3 miles into a commercial dock, in a protected cove, within a protected bay. We are moored now to the unmoving shore. We shall indeed sleep a different sleep tonight.

CHAPTER

13

Path Between the Seas

Day Thirteen—Balboa City, Panama: The guns are silent now, but the very brief war is still first on the minds of the people. Government employees, such as those checking our passports at the gate, or the postal clerk, who took my U.S. dollar for a stamp, seem quite serious. Not hostile at all, but serious. But others along the dock who have time to talk were eager to tell of the liberation our country had given them. "Oh, it was the only way; we could not have thrown 'them' out ourselves. Now we can openly talk again without fear."

And John Mercier, the most articulate *and* informed Admeasurer, who came aboard, promptly at 0800 hrs to measure our ships for cargo capacity, the basis for charges for passage, was also most emphatic about the relief their re-found freedom has given them. He was also remarkably informed on the operation and maintenance of this crucial waterway, and he highly recommended a book, *Path Between The Seas*. The book researches the French attempts at the building, the American success, and the sub-

We quietly wait our turn to take that historic
Path Between The Seas in Balboa Harbor, Panama.

sequent engineering studies aimed at enlarging the present locks to the possibility of a sea-level Canal here. I shall surely research that book.

But for now, let me again quote from Publication 153, Defense Maritime Agency: "9.09 General remarks.—The Panama Canal, a lock type canal, connects the Pacific Ocean with the Atlantic Ocean running in a general N.W. direction from Balboa on the S side to Crystobal on the N side. The greatest part of the canal is at the level of Gatun Lake, which varies from 25 to 26.5 m (82 to 87 ft.) above sea level according to the season of the year. Gatun Lake is reached through three sets of locks, which are arranged in duplicate on either side of the most elevated part of the canal."

As previously stated, Capt. Wengel told me that the usual expression of the "length" of the canal is, "49 miles from sea to sea."

I was surprised to find such a tide range here, 18 feet; but when Mercier explained it, I realized that I should have thought of the principle involved. The Gulf of Panama presents a concave shore to the sea. The tide, produced principally by the gravitational pull of the moon, is actually two approximately 12,000-mile-long waves, racing around the globe at close to 1000 miles per hour. Because of that tremendouse length, however, we see it as just a "rising tide," or a "falling tide." Of course it produces some flow, in the inlets, but the tide itself is really a wave.

And that concave shore focuses that wave energy almost directly on the western end of this Canal. The wave is narrowed, restricted; and that, of course, markedly increases its height, locally. And conversely, the eastern end, where the shoreline presents a convex curve, the tide is about 18 inches.

And that is all, I think, that we need to say about tides, on our long run to Puerto Rico.

1130 hrs: Refueling for our hungry Jimmys has been completed; the Captain is in town procuring a few more stores for our 2½- day run, and one-day cleanup of our ships in Puerto Rico; and I am guarding the ships, after a pleasant, half mile walk under the hot sun, along a busy thoroughfare to the post office. I was pleasantly surprised that the clerk readily took my U.S. currency for my stamps.

1730 hrs: The Pilot aboard, we slipped our lines, and started north along this famous water "Path-

Puerto de Balboa, Republic de Panama.

way." We photographed each other's ships against the tropic background, and entered the first set of locks, just as we lost the sunlight for the day.

Capt. Wengel had tried to gain us a daytime passage, but the heavy traffic would not allow. We shall rush through the famed Gailard Cut; we shall race across the world known Gatun Lake; we shall drop down through the Gatun Locks to the level of the eastern seas, all in the dark of night.

Oh, I have written much about the beauty in the night; I have spent thousands of hours at the wheel of a tug or patrol boat, in the gentle, peaceful, dark of the night. But I think I shall not pass this way again. It would have been good to have seen it in the light of day. Still, would I sell the rich experience of this voyage? No, not for any price.

We shall drop our hooks in Cristobal Harbor about 0300 hrs, wait for the day, and then, and then, pray; if not for "fair winds and following seas," at least for light headwinds and low seas. At dawn, we shall point our bows east-northeastward, for our final, long, 900-mile run, out across the middle of the Caribbean Sea to the future home port of these racing catamarans.

And we shall not be cruising under the lee of the Leeward and Windward Islands, but will be challenging the western waters of this open sea, where, for 900 miles, the waves will have had a chance to build under the push of the prevailing east wind. We shall pray, as we hang at anchor in Cristobal Harbor, for light headwinds and low seas. And we shall accept, with deep gratitude, if it be in the Divine Plan, those "fair winds, and following seas."

2130 hrs: One hour and fifteen minutes across Gatun Lake to the Gatun Locks. The Pilot, a huge, vigorous man in his sixties, just told us, "This is the fastest trip I have *ever* made between these two sets of locks. I have Piloted some 26-knot ships through here, but they could not build up their speed, and then drop it down again, and 'average' that."

A very observant man, he noted the excellent aluminum welds. I used the opportunity to give him my Nichols Sales Representative card, and invite him for a tour of the yard, if he is ever in Washington State. Again, I told him, "Tell my cousin, Matt, the President, that Dean said Matt would give you a *personal* tour." He was delighted. These unique, masterfully crafted small ships do catch the eye of the observing.

There are five or six ships waiting for lockage, but the Pilot said that, because we are small, we shall lock through with the first ship.

And an hour or so later, we did. And now, 0100 hrs, April 11, we are at anchor in the roadstead of Cristobal. We sail eastward at dawn.

CHAPTER 14

Diversion to Paradise

Day Fourteen—0600 hrs: Wakeup call, as this most interesting mix between Captain, and Navy Chief Bos'n, swept through the ship. "Let's get moving, men; looks like it's going to kick us around out there today; let's get at it—and let's clean this ship up. It's getting to look like a pigpen."

He was right, of course. A bit direct, but he was right. I like men, and I like being a man. But I have found, over the long years, that, without a woman around, men, especially young men, tend to become slobs. Oh, they snapped to when the order was given and quickly cleaned up the ship.

"Look here," that Chief Bos'n hammered, "Look at this table. ___ all over it, and a garbage bag not a foot away."

The old banana-peel-syndrome, I think. These otherwise competent, capable, personable young men would drop a wrapper, or a peeling on the table. And of course, the next man would not touch it. "I didn't put it there; why should I pick it up?" was the thought, if they thought of it at all. Often, I found myself picking up after them, and I'm sure no one noticed. Nor did I care. These are otherwise competent, capable, personable, young men. I would sail with them any day.

0800 hrs: We pass the breakwater at Cristobal, and enter the Caribbean Sea; and are met with freshening winds, and building, 4- to 6-foot seas. It could be a long ride to Puerto Rico.

It is curious, but I do not feel as though we are on the last leg of this journey, but rather that we are on a whole new voyage. We are no longer on the west coast of the Americas; we are in a whole new sea; and we travel no more southward, but northeastward across the open sea. Less than a thousand miles, but it could be a long road to Puerto Rico.

0900 hrs: We are in deeper water; the swells have lengthened, easing that part of the ride. There are still 2 to 4 foot seas on top, also from dead ahead, but they have not worsened. The Cats handle the swells well. If the seas do not worsen, we *could* have a tolerable ride to Puerto Rico.

I had not thought of the Caribbean as being mean, but she is baring her teeth a bit this morning. Atlantic storms; Pacific gales, yes; but except for the roaring hurricanes, surely, not so with the gentle Caribbean. I am learning a new lesson today. I think that when we clear the Los Fallarones shallows, on this north coast of Panama, and get into truly deeper waters, the swells, at least, should lengthen even more. But the term "brutal" is coming again to mind.

0945 hrs: The ride has worsened. The two-gallon water jug came off the water cooler, and started around the deck; the five pound, brass nozzle on a fire hose hit the deck with a bang; a cover over one of the air conditioner thermostats, hit the deck with a crack; several items flew off the "galley" table. I'm sure the Pacific can be wild, but she never gave us anything so brutal as this.

The Captain just ordered RPMs reduced to 1600. A wise move I think.

1100 hrs: We have reduced our RPMs now to 1500. Even so, the head sea and swell combinations must combine at times to 12 feet or higher. And it seems their length must be close to the 76 feet of our hulls; for once in a while, the entire ship leaps up, and forward, and then drops straight down into the trough. When 10 to 20 tons of Caribbean sea water slams up under that forward deck, thunder explodes up there, and sends a shudder, perhaps I should say, a bruising shock through the entire ship. It *is* brutal. Exhilarating, but brutal. And even yet, if he was so inclined, a man could cook in the microwave—if he was so inclined.

1230 hrs: The generator set on our ship shut down. Instruments indicate low oil pressure, but the engine oil is full. The Engineer thinks that a safety shutdown sensor has over reacted from this pounding. The Captain has decided to turn and run for a small island group, about 30 miles off our starboard beam, where we can find shelter, secure the *San Geronimo* alongside, and trouble shoot the problem in quiet water. The sea asks no quarter; she gives none.

1415 hrs: "All things work together for good, to them who love God...." So speaks the Good Book. We are side by side, nosed into the white, sand beach of

Two battlers of the open sea rest but for a little while snug against the sands of Chichime, San Blas Islands, Panama.

the island of Chichime in the San Blas Island group, off the shores of Panama. There is no motion in the firm deck beneath our feet. Friendly natives literally smile at us from the doorway of their grass house, 30 feet off our bow. Behind us, in the brilliant, green waters of the lagoon, that is formed by the two islands called Chichime and the reef between them, three cruising sailboats rest at anchor. They are 30 to 40 footers, two sloops, and a ketch. The thick groves of palm trees that cover each half mile long island crowd to the white, sand beach.

Rex, Engineer from the *San Geronimo*, is certain that he can correct our generator problem, but of course, in the meantime, I think I'll take a swim in the warm, green waters of a lovely lagoon behind an island in the Caribbean Sea.

Diversion to Paradise

Home beside the sea, Chichime, San Blas Islands, Panama.

Capt. Bob believes he is the first of today's cruisers to discover a way through the barrier reefs to this lagoon. In 1982, with another Nichols-built ship, the *Great Rivers Explorer*, he nosed carefully around and found the channel. And today, it has given us shelter and a time of peace to find healing for our ship, and, of course, a rare opportunity to turn the "brutal" ride aside for yet a little while and swim, and refresh ourselves in this tiny corner of paradise.

1930 hrs: Music, sweet music—from the low, tropical island, under the sighing palm trees? No, from the engine room of one Cat of two for Puerto Rico. Our generator plant coughed, caught, died, and then came to life with its own steady purr.

Rex, with Kurt sweating with him in that oven of an engine room, had pretty much isolated the problem down to a faulty, engine cutoff solenoid. They removed the entire fuel pump unit, and got it on the cooler deck. But the instruction manual said only, in effect, "At that point, get a new pump." But we were possibly several thousand miles from a new pump.

(True, as the Captain, and two Engineers literally "sweat it out," the rest of us were diving off the stern into those warm, green waters of this tropical lagoon, and buying shells from the tiny people, the Cuna Indians. But we are *not* on a "cruise.")

So the Captain got on the radio, called the Marine Operator; and from here, in this far away place, was soon talking to Jeff Binford at the Nichols Yard in N.W. Washington State. Jeff had some suggestions, but the best one was the telephone number of the John Deere people in Seattle. Capt. Bob called; and a very knowledgeable technician, or Engineer came on, explained more details, asked good questions, and then gave permission to open up a warranted part.

And that opening up only proved that there was no fault in the pump or cutoff solenoid. The problem *had* to be in the wiring supplying power to that solenoid. So they re-installed that pump, down in that furnace of an engine room, jury-rigged a power supply wire direct from the batteries to the switch. The engine ran. But the so brief twilight of the tropics had come and gone. It was very dark.

"No, we will not sail tonight," an energetic, yet cautious Captain told us, "I know that channel, alright, but I need light to see the reefs. We'll sail at first light."

Diversion to Paradise

The old and the new. Yet both serve man today upon the still yet moving sea. Chichime, San Blas Islands, Panama.

When we lost our generator at noon, Capt. Bob had turned us about 90 degrees to the right, and we ran the 25 miles or so to these lovely islands. Tomorrow at dawn, as soon as we clear the reefs, we will take a new course, at a very shallow angle, and intercept our original course a 100 miles or so east. We have lost 18 hours, and about 30 miles. But our ships are still sailing, and we have been blessed that, if a problem must arise, that it arose when it did. We shall sleep tonight, washed clean by the salty sea, and listening to the "music" of a generator set, as we nuzzle the beach in a warm, tropical lagoon.

CHAPTER 15

Brutal

Day Fifteen—"Dean, I'm going to have to move you over to the *Geronimo*. We have no generator, and we must sail without it. Conditions on this ship will no longer be austere; they will be primitive. With no generator, there will be no toilets, no cooking, and we will have very limited battery power. I'll have my hands full navigating. With you over there, I'll have one less man here to worry about."

I understood, of course, and moved over to the open space on the deck, aft of the last row of seats, on the *San Geronimo*.

It had been a lovely, peaceful, healing night, even though I'd found myself up around 0200 hrs redoing some lines. The slight tide had lifted the *Geronimo* off the beach; she had shifted just a bit, so that the two metal guard rails up forward were thumping together now and then. The old tugboatman in me couldn't stand that. So I slipped out, in just my shorts, into the deep dusk of this warm, tropic night, and let the light, warm, tradewinds caress my bare skin.

I slacked off the forward line, holding the two ships together, so that the *Geronimo* could lay square alongside; and then took up the aft line to keep her there. Now, there is but the occasional squeak of the fender tires. But that is a sound that should be there. That does not disturb sleep.

But the only shoreline was the bowline from the *San Juan* to a palm tree, 75 feet away. There was a light set to the tide from our left; but generally, the light breeze from our right kept the two ships square with the beach. As I stood there, drinking in the peace and beauty of the night that light breeze slacked off and that light set of the tide pushed the two ships to the right. I could see that with just a bit more push that the now slightly slacked bowline *could* allow us to buckle around and lay the *San Juan* broadside to the beach. Oh, no harm would be done in this secure and unhurried place. But it would just be better if we could remain firmly nose on to the beach. So I just waited, enjoying the solitude in that pleasant, tropic night. And presently, the breeze picked up, and nudged our two ships square with the beach again; that bowline slacked off; and I took up 2 or 3 feet of slack, and went back to bed. There had been no cause to call any other crew out. Sometimes it is good to work with lines alone on a peaceful night aboard a boat on the sea.

But why had we no generator?

0600 hrs: The Captain called a sleepy crew from our bunks. And ashore, under the palm trees, a rooster crowed. How could there be trouble in such a peaceful place?

But last evening, just as he shut down for the night, Kurt had noticed oil had blown out of a breather pipe.

"Well, let's go to bed. We'll check it in the morning," the Captain wisely said.

And in the morning, Kurt found the oil level in that generator motor very high. He drained out the excess, but also found the cause. Diesel fuel was getting by a seal in the fuel pump and diluting the lubricating oil in the engine base. An intolerable condition. So, trouble has won that round; we sail, afterall, with no generator.

And just before 0800 hrs, two subdued crews sailed two small ships out through the reefs that protected that peaceful place and into the seas, forecast to 12 to 15 feet, and winds forecast to 25 knots, all on the nose.

1200 hrs: It is brutal. Under a 3000 ft., heavy overcast, we push on, at some reduced speed, but still at 16 knots into the forecast 15 foot, short, steep seas. Sometimes the shuddering slams send shocks into my body, there on that six-inch foam mattress. And one time, in the head, both my feet came 6 to 8 inches off the deck. When 60 tons of boat comes off a 15-foot wave, and slams down upon 60 tons of sea water, the sea hardly notices; but the resulting shock is felt in every metal fibre of this ship. Is it possible that even these marvelous craft are being asked to do more than they were designed to do?

1500 hrs: If these seas are not "mountainous," they are some mighty rugged hills. We are pitching fore and aft at least 30 degrees, perhaps more, from nose down to nose up. The *San Juan*, cruising a comfortable distance off our starboard bow, took a big, green one over their bow. They cut their engines, of course, but the ship took a shear to the left, and

Through our own wet glass, we see our tiny sister ship climbing a mountain of sea.

across our bow. George Ott got us stopped, but only feet from their side. As someone laconically said, "That's the sort of action that is not in the script."

1600 hrs: I truly pray that these Nichols-built boats are as tough as their reputation says they are; for they are indeed taking a brutal pounding. Frequently, there are breaking seas out there, real combers. Stephan, on the *San Juan*, had gone out on their foredeck to re-secure their boarding ladder. He was thrown, someway, and broke or badly sprained his wrist.

1630 hrs: We are at half speed. But the head seas are so steep and short, we still frequently slam that forward, flat underbelly down on that momentarily solid, green water. The thunderous shock through the ship is formidable.

We shall sleep in our clothes tonight.

CHAPTER

16

And Yet Brutal

Day Sixteen—0400 hrs: We are at idle speed to give our Engineer less motion to contend with as he checks his engine room. A full moon casts its ever lovely, yellow path across a lovely sea. A few brilliant stars join the heavenly display. Such innocence, such peaceful innocence, as we rest here these few moments. But we have an appointment with time in Puerto Rico. And so we open up our engines, and the battle rages on.

Dawn: And two determined Cats yet fight and claw their way, driving their bows over an angry sea toward the rising sun.

0930 hrs: The ship is becoming a shambles. Besides the sloppy housekeeping of a delightfully young crew, but with their casual attitudes toward such things, the incredible bucking, pitching, and rocking of this light, aluminum can, has tossed items onto the deck; items there are thrown around. I managed to comb my hair, although I may have parted it in two places. Unable to divert the energy to the struggle it would be, just to change clothes, we

Angry seas leaving the Panama Canal heading ENE. Note the reflection in the side glass.

are increasingly aware of our dirty, and sweaty clothes and bodies. Every move is a struggle. And I notice that we all are just a bit reluctant to move. Spontaneous initiative is not there. We must will our bodies to move.

A 50-gallon water barrel, poorly lashed, is still standing next to its post, but it has slid around that post at least 90 degrees.

And that is something curious about these otherwise eager, capable young men—their line handling, and anchor drill are atrocious. Don't the older men teach the young men anymore? Or won't the young ones listen? And why always, always the back turn. Lads, if you don't have enough bends on the cleat to hold without that back turn, it is only a matter of time until you will be taking that line off one day with an axe or a knife. That backturn should be there *only* to hold an unattended line in place; *never* to keep the line from slipping on the bit.

And the securing of these two small ships, side by side, to the seawall in Acapulco made me almost cry. Two spring lines, and two breast lines, lads, if correctly done, that is enough. And when you have a tide, make them as long as possible. And where there is a surge, as at Acapulco, wrap your lines, or fair lead them so there is no chafe. We nearly lost one one-inch "poly" line from chafe there. A wise old man is one who has learned much over his long years. A wise young man is one who will learn from the wise old man. Oh, but I would sail with these young men any day.

I lost my own beautiful and only son to the sea, off Anchor Point, Alaska in November of 1966. The poignant memory of that loss still tears at my heart, and touches the corners of my eyes. Oh yes, I would be proud to call any one of these fine lads my son.

But here, in the heart of the Caribbean, for now, we are simply surviving a run across a sea that asks no quarter and gives none—and we are again doing so at 20 knots. We shall clean up tomorrow.

1300 hrs: It is not "smoother" now, but it *is* less rough. We welcome the easier ride. The ocean must be deeper again here, because the swells are a bit longer. And the headwinds must have slackened just a bit, because the seas are not as high and steep.

I know that I just referred to this water as an ocean. And I know that a look at a map of the world will show the Caribbean to be even one of the smaller seas, smaller even than the Gulf of Mexico.

But here, with no land from horizon to horizon, and after the incredibly rough beating we have endured for the last 24 hours, I think I may use a writer's license and call this an ocean today.

Garrett Terwilliger just told me that the Captain gave us an ETA of around 1700 tomorrow. The Caribbean, so far, has not stopped us, but her resistance to our passing has cost us many hours. We would have to confess that, with her shallower waters, her shorter swells, her steeper seas, the Caribbean has given us 24 hard hours, pushing our ships and crowding the design plans of their creators.

1700 hrs: The seas and winds have lessened. They are still moving, but we are again loping easily along upon a peaceful sea.

CHAPTER 17

The Taste of Victory

Day Seventeen—"And man shall have dominion over the land [and sea]...."

But He did not say it would be easy. In fact, it is indeed, "by the sweat of his brow," the fatigue of his body, the bruising of his arms and legs, the testing, the trying of his will.

This is no "downhill run to Bora Bora," but indeed, an uphill climb to Puerto Rico.

Dawn: And the Caribbean again resists our passing. It is difficult to keep pen on paper, and then to read what was written. The turbulent sea has entered its hand also.

We had spoken earlier of this last leg seeming more like a whole, new voyage. But the severe resistance we have received has made it seem even more like an invasion. But the war is over, sea. We are legally here. We are Americans, delivering two American ships from one American Port to another. And besides, it is written, "Man *shall* have dominion...."

But the sea has a tremendous advantage; she is a tireless sea. Nine very weary sailors just hang on and wait. Our engines have fuel, and as long as they have fuel, they too are tireless. And so, as man wills, the governors remain at 1700 RPMs, and we press northeastward toward our landfall tonight.

But the sailors? There is little conversation; there is limited movement about; the off-watch crews almost immediately hit their bunks; personal grooming is minimal; and all are clinging, in hope, to the vision of seeing ourselves standing tonight in a cascading shower and letting that rushing stream wash away the salt, and the sweat, and the grime, and yes, the tension and fatigue. Yes, man can conquer the sea; but he does so by wit, and will, and cunning, but most of all, by the Grace of God.

0915 hrs: It is a glorious day, with only scattered clouds in a dusty, blue sky. Two islands, one small, one perhaps 3 or 4 miles long, appear off our starboard bow. Our determined, and resourceful young Captain, using his years of experience and his knowledge of the sea should have an opportunity to update his DR position.

1130 hrs: Borinquen Point, on the N.W. corner of the West Indies island of Puerto Rico, rises out of the sea haze off our starboard bow. It is one hundred miles or so yet eastward to our harbor, but this is the island in the sea that we have been reaching for for 5,500 miles, and 17 long days.

1300 hrs: We are in the Atlantic Ocean now. And still the seas off the north shores of Puerto Rico resist our passing. And south of us, along the ridge of this island, as far as we can see, east and west, a wall of towering cumulus clouds mark the center mountain range of this island.

And the *San Juan* just radioed for Rex. They are losing power on their port engine. And that was serious. To lose an engine could quite possibly mean losing a ship. These rigs are just not equipped for towing, nor are these crews skilled for towing, especially in these turbulent seas. They could run for the shore, and save their lives; but they could lose the ship.

But whether Rex's serious and wise council helped or not, they got her back to full power. Hang on, faithful Jimmy, hang on for yet a few more hours. We are almost there. And the sea answers with increased winds and higher seas.

1500 hrs: Again, the *San Juan* radioed for Rex. "We are losing power again on our port engine." And again, the quiet, serious council by Rex, to Kurt, the Engineer on the *San Juan*, suggested the switching of some valves, to put the engine on a different tank; and that faithful Jimmy, cleared her throat, and picked up her full power again. The crushing seas earlier had destroyed a "sounding tube" to the "day tank," a smaller tank used intermittently. Without that sounding tube, the remaining fuel had to be estimated. If there was less fuel than their estimate, then the terrible turbulence, Rex reasoned, was foaming up the diesel fuel in that smaller, day tank. The switching of tanks would give that engine solid fuel again, was his reasoning. It seemed to work. But every member of both crews was praying, in their own, unique ways, perhaps, but praying, "C'mon, baby, hang on, hang on, we're almost there; hang on baby."

1630 hrs: We did it; we did it. We are secured to a nondescript pier, in a narrow, shallow, muddy slough, but we have won over the angry sea. Until we turned into the entrance to San Juan Harbor, the angry seas fought us. And then, if we can call it that, we made our twin, racing runs down the middle of San Juan Harbor, past the multi-million dollar cruise ships, past the piers, and multi-million dollar condos, and office buildings.

One would have thought they would dock us in the heart of town, just beneath the Governor's Mansion. But instead, we are tucked away in this muddy, backwater slough of San Juan Harbor. But one thing they cannot take from us—the rich taste of victory. We battled 5,500 miles of ocean, and canal, and sea, and another ocean, and we have won.

And as we made that racing run, secure in the calm waters, away from that tempestuous sea, I was not surprised to hear the subdued but relief filled voices of at least two of the crewmen say, "Thank You Lord, thank You. You brought us through; You really brought us through."

It has been written, "Eight times out of ten, the skilled hand is the lucky one." Or, as the oldtimers used to say, "God helps them who help themselves."

But more accurately, I believe with all my heart that we all indeed are granted, each day, a certain amount of Heavenly Grace. If we persist in overdrawing that account, our Guardian Angels will, one day, demand an accounting.

Over these seventeen, packed full days, I have watched a real Captain, an indominable Navy Chief Bos'n, push his Guardian Angel to the limit; but so far as I can see, he has not yet overdrawn his account.

I think that the next time I have three million dollars worth of ships to send across the seas somewhere, I'll call that tough, old Navy Chief Bos'n, and say, "Take 'em, Capt. Bob; they're all yours. And by the way, be sure and take along as many of that same, delightful, motley crew as you can."

And now, two docile Cats rest quietly at this nondescript quay in a backwater slough of San Juan Harbor. Their engines stilled, they patiently wait their next command from a new Captain, and a new crew. And they will, as tirelessly as for us, respond— well, or poorly, in direct proportion to the skills of their new commanders.

Home in the backwaters of San Juan Harbor, Puerto Rico.

We will be parting soon, scattering like the spray from a wave, when it meets the shore. People, I have found, are fluid, like the sea. They flow together when, whatever confines them, holds them close. But when that confining is removed, they drift apart, as the sea water drifts and flows away when its confines are removed.

We nine, but especially we five aboard this small ship, have grown together these seventeen days and over 5000 miles of our voyage. We have learned each others step, his interests, his sense of humor, his tolerances, (and intolerances, although among this crew, they were nearly nil). We have learned, in a quite limited way, of course, but we have learned to love each other as brothers, in a common family.

As there should be, there will be some rending, small, perhaps, but some rending at the parting. And we shall miss our faithful steeds, whose metal sides and decks, whose plastic seats, and clinical heads, were our common homes. And we shall even miss the ceaseless, rumbling, purr of their engines, that became so much a part of our lives we noticed only when they changed speeds.

We have built a common memory; we have shared a common adventure; we have won a common victory. Down the long years, should we meet again, the bonds of that sharing will draw us into a rich and common "remembering."

We are eager to fly home. But there will be some rending at the parting, even though the only thing that drew us together was to deliver Two Cats To Puerto Rico.

www.ingramcontent.com/pod-product-compliance
Lightning Source LLC
Chambersburg PA
CBHW070508090426
42735CB00012B/2697